TABLE OF CONTENTS

America has come so far since its beginning. There have been many great discoveries, groundbreaking inventions, and productive innovations that have given rise to some of the greatest wealth our nation has known. This has come to define what the American Dream is all about. It is the desire to develop a product, an idea, or even a procedure and then be able to uniquely package that commodity to make a profit in our free-market society.

As Americans, when we are faced with over-whelming odds, the challenge becomes something we aspire to. This obstacle produces a pathway to greatness, not an excuse for a lack of achievement. It is what many Americans before us have attained and what has inspired so many people to excel in their own lives. So many opportunities have been created for our citizens as we have taken on those challenges and won. From the making of peanut butter, to setting up assembly lines, to putting the first man on the moon, we have continually striven to be first and to be the best.

This book is written because of the passion that we Americans have, but a passion we are losing. Ever in-creasing social programs, unfair restrictions on business-es, stifling effects of worker's unions, increased taxation on businesses and individuals, and increased government debt obligations have created a situation that we must reverse. If we do not, we risk losing our place as an economic leader. We must right this ship or we will sink further into the quagmire of mediocrity.

I want to address many issues that I feel we miss when discussing how we can turn this economy around.

Although we may not agree on all these points, I believe they are valid and should open discussions about things we have failed to talk about before. At the very heart of any economic issue we discuss is the question of "How do we create jobs?". The first section of this book is dedicated to several ideas that should take center-stage. Businesses today are hindered from growing because of the many burdens they carry when it comes to hiring employees. Over and over again, as a small business owner, I hear other owners talk about the reasons they do not hire employees. The bottom line is that it is too expensive and there are too many regulations that make hiring employees not worth the hassle.

A story I use to illustrate this point is one of Alexander Graham Bell and the invention of the telephone. It goes something like this: if Mr. Bell were trying to invent the telephone today, he would have to hire Watson at minimum wage and pay him overtime if he worked more than 40 hours in a week. He would have to withhold Federal, State, Social Security, and Medicare taxes from Watson's paycheck and submit it monthly. He would also have to match the other half of Watson's Social Security and Medicare taxes himself. In addition to that, he would have to pay Unemployment Insurance to the State and to the Federal Government. Then he would have to carry worker's compensation insurance in case Watson was injured. Liability insurance is needed to cover his vehicle should he be involved in an accident on the way across town to pick up the telephone on the other end. This doesn't include any oversight from federal agencies such as OSHA or the FCC or any local governmental fees that may be assessed. All of this before the telephone has even been invented. Given this scenario, I don't know that the telephone could be invented here in America today.

The costs listed in the paragraph above illustrate many of the reasons various companies will choose to manufacture in countries where employment is much less expensive and regulations favor businesses instead of hindering them. However, it is my belief that most of the American businesses who manufacture outside of the U.S. do so, not because they want to, but because they have to. There are just too many expenses that they have to contend with here that they do not have to worry about elsewhere. In order to keep jobs here we will have to change many of the costs and regulations that employers face.

This is a real problem that we must fix and in a most expeditious way. Unless we do, we will become a nation that has failed to lead. Our dollar will continue to be devalued, our citizens will lose their jobs, and we will find it much more difficult to recover our esteemed place as an economic hub.

BUSINESS TAXES

Various local taxes are assessed to businesses that are not assessed to individuals. There may be an inventory tax, higher property taxes because of commercial zoning, business permits, etc. and these taxes take money out of the business. When that money is used to pay taxes it cannot be used to hire employees, increase production, advertise, or do other essential business functions that lead to growth. Bit-by-bit and chunk-by-chunk they eat away at our businesses.

It is now time for each state and local area to examine and eliminate any extra taxes or fees on businesses. Permits, licenses, etc. must be made very reasonable. This will help the entrepreneurs just beginning and established businesses to continue operating.

Business personal property taxes should be eliminated. This would allow companies to purchase the equipment necessary to operate without a tax consequence. Shelving, computers, chairs, and so on, purchased by a business not only creates other jobs but are a regular part of doing business. These items should not be taxed as personal property. Again, let the companies use this money to create more jobs and give them extra finances so they can more readily expand.

A question we must ask ourselves is why do we make it harder for businesses to survive when they are the backbone of our economy. We must remove those taxes and other frivolous fees from our job creation centers. Until we do, we will continue to burden our employers to the point of going out of business or relocating out of the country.

Another area to consider because of the current economic climate is that of businesses who are delinquent on their taxes. Many of these businesses did well to survive the initial downturn and tried to stay open. Many have employees they did not want to lay off because they thought, and hoped, the economy was going to turn around more quickly than it did.

These owners considered the welfare of their employees and their families and held onto them thinking things would get better. Many found themselves late on payroll taxes and sales taxes. Late taxes can smother businesses with all the fees and penalties that are assessed. Even though many of these business survived the hardest part of the downturn they now find themselves struggling and shuttering because of these tax debts.

We should have a one-time waiver of these taxes that are delinquent to allow the business to survive. This may not seem fair to the other businesses that have struggled to maintain a good standing with the government. But, the fact remains that if a company closes and the workers are left unemployed it does not help the economy. We must address this issue as the loss of more jobs does not seem acceptable to me.

MINIMUM WAGE

One of the biggest mistakes we make is when we refer to the "minimum wage" as equivalent to a "livable wage." My definition for the minimum wage is a price-point that does not allow the employer to take advantage of the employee. A minimum wage should not be intended or promoted as a livable wage. A person can live on this amount but may need to work more hours or have a supplemental job.

I know there are several small business owners who do pay the minimum wage to their employees and yet fail to make minimum wage themselves, considering the hours invested. Late nights, weekends, and phone calls on the holidays are all part of a business owner's routine. As their business grows and they add employees, expenses go up. Many owners find that they still make less than minimum wage on an hour-for-hour work-week.

Many of these small businesses will shutter. The owners finally get to the point where they see that they can make more money, have more time off, and have more benefits by becoming an employee again. Unfortunately, when this happens, the workers at that small business lose their jobs and the local economy suffers.

The minimum wage has long been a pawn in a challenging game of political chess. In order to gain more votes, politicians appeal to this large block of voters by promising higher wages through increases in the minimum wage. These higher costs of operating must be absorbed by the company or passed on to the consumer through higher prices.   Instead of focusing on increasing the minimum wage, it would be nice if politicians worked on retaining the jobs that are leaving our beloved country and workers behind.

Typically, jobs that pay a minimum wage are offered by companies that hire unskilled laborers or small companies trying to gain a foothold in their market. These companies usually have little wiggle room for wage increases because of their market, type of hires, and current income levels.   There are many small businesses that cannot even afford the current minimum wage required by law, especially when employment taxes are figured into the equation..

When minimum wage levels increase these companies will usually do three things. First, they will evaluate the need for the amount of employees they have been operating with. During this phase they will usually fire under-performers. They may have kept some sub-par employees and let them continue earning a paycheck at old wage levels but find it very bad business to pay them even more for mediocre work. Second, they will look for ways to increase the cost of their products or services that the customers purchase. Consumers, especially employees that make minimum wage, now make a higher wage but are charged more for groceries, clothing, and household supplies as businesses increase prices in an attempt to stay profitable. The third thing employers do is refocus their business to the more productive lines. When doing this they consider lines that may have low profit margins which will now be squeezed even tighter. They have to make a choice of whether to keep it or shut it down. If some of those lines are eliminated then the workers find themselves unemployed.

Increasing the minimum wage does one thing for sure: it artificially increases the cost of doing business. It is not conducive to supply and demand economics. In our recession-like economy, minimum wage is at what I consider a high level. At this level it removes the ability for businesses to adjust to decreasing demand and may have even contributed to the loss of many businesses in our country and the jobs they created.

I am not completely against a minimum wage as I know there are employers in certain areas and situations which could take advantage of a group of employees. Perhaps they are the only employer, or one of a very few employers, in an area where jobs are so scarce that people will work for nearly anything to support their families. This is one example in which a situation exists that makes having a minimum wage useful. There may be other situations also but I am hard pressed to find very many.

I would like to see the minimum wage start to decrease back to lower levels. This should be a steady but slow decrease so that prices may adjust, as to not tremendously hurt the supply/demand cycle.

The bad part about trying to decrease this wage is there are many adjustments that have already been made in prices that will not easily be undone. Everything from property taxes, real estate taxes, home rent, etc. will need to decrease in conjunction with the lowering of the mini-mum wage. That will be the hardest part of the equation to deal with because, as I pointed out earlier, imposing a minimum wage artificially increases other costs. A house that should rent for $300 per month rents for $400 per month. A bottle of cola is priced at $1.25 when it should be $1.00. Concert tickets that sell for $50 when they should be $30.

It is because of all these other prices that it is harder to deal with this problem. We would be foolish to think that all of this can be undone rapidly without a major collapse in our economy. If we begin lowering the minimum wage it will need to be done with steady, planned cuts and not with just wholesale chopping. Prices didn't rise overnight and they surely will not go down that way either.

I know in my business, I do not have even one employee who works for minimum wage. This is because I understand that I must pay more to keep good, knowledgeable, and experienced workers. I assume that there are many employers who, through experience, do the same thing. The wages they pay will not be affected by this change.

There are, however, some services I would like to add in my business. After a study of the cost feasibility, including paying employees minimum wage, I find that there would not be enough profit for me to justify venturing into them. I have considered using my staff I have employed now to do the additional jobs, but it would be more work than they could handle efficiently. So, those ideas for business growth and opportunity sit on the shelf - no jobs are created and no profit is made.

What we need to do now is look to our future and the future of those who will inherit what we leave behind. Let us start to correct the problems associated with the minimum wage before they get much further out of hand. We need to let the market determine wages and not the government. If we do that, we will start to see prices go down and working people will be able to afford the goods and services we have to offer. Let us get back to true supply and demand economics.

NEGOTIATED WAGES

When I was 17 years old I moved about an hour-and-a-half away from my parents, rented a small apartment, and went to work at a convenience store three midnight shifts a week. I found myself needing some extra income so I went to work for a mom-and-pop video rental store as a second job. It was in a small town and although minimum wage was $3.35 an hour, they told me they could not afford to pay that amount and instead offered me $2.50 an hour. I was also told about the fringe benefit of being able to take movies home to watch for free (as long as they were not heavily rented titles.) This was one benefit that did me no good at all since I was not much of a movie buff and between both jobs I did well to get the much needed sleep I needed. I took the job because I needed the extra money and I was thankful for it. The work was not hard and I felt that although it was not very good pay, I was satisfied with it for the kind of work I was expected to do.

There are many businesses that are in that same situation. They would like to hire some employees but feel they cannot afford to do so because they cannot pay the minimum wage. I propose that companies with five or fewer employees be exempt from the minimum wage and overtime laws. We should let the employers negotiate with the employees in those small companies and agree on acceptable terms that both parties feel is fair to them.

Some may say that many employers will stop paying their employees much at all because of this. I disagree. You can't hire someone for nothing and you will not get someone to work for much less money if they know they can go elsewhere and make significantly more. Employers will want to keep good employees and will pay more, if possible, to keep those who truly are a benefit to the company.

I believe that if you give employers this option there are many who will begin to hire people they are not hiring now. As long as the employee feels he or she is being compensated enough for the job offered, both parties are happy with the terms, then a beneficial relationship is formed. Our government should not hinder this arrangement.

COLLECTING PAYROLL TAXES

When employees receive their paychecks they are often surprised by how many taxes are withheld and sent to the state and to the federal government. Many of these employees wait all year and then receive their W2 forms, prepare their tax forms, submit them to the state and the Internal Revenue Service, and wait for their refund check to come in.

There are many people who work for wages below the level required to pay income taxes. The refund they receive is usually for the entire amount of taxes withheld from their checks (excluding Social Security and Medicare taxes).

The problem with this procedure is it takes money away from the workers that, if working for a low wage, they would be able to use for everyday living expenses. Low-wage earners do not need to wait an entire year to receive this money while the government uses it interest-free.

There is a part of the IRS W4 Form that allows low-income earners to abstain from having federal taxes withheld from their paychecks. This is how the IRS describes the process on its website: *If an employee qualifies, Form W-4 is also used by the employee to tell you not to deduct any Federal income tax from his or her wages. To qualify for this exempt status, the employee must have had no tax liability for the previous year and must expect to have no tax liability for the current year.*

However, if the employee can be claimed as a dependent on a parent's or another person's tax return, additional limitations may apply. See the instructions for Form W-4. A Form W-4 claiming exemption from withholding is valid for only one calendar year. To continue to be exempt from withholding in the next year, an employee must give you a new Form W-4 claiming exempt status by February 15 of that year. If the employee does not give you a new Form W-4, withhold tax as if he or she is single, with no withholding allowances. However, if you have an earlier Form W-4 (not claiming exempt status) for this employee that is valid, withhold as you did before.

That seems very clear, doesn't it? We need to simplify this process and better identify employees who will benefit from this exemption. Let us determine a certain income level that will allow employers and employees to know for sure that they are exempt. Currently, the IRS levies a $500 fine on anyone who files for the exemption and then earns enough to incur a tax liability. It is because of the arbitrary wording that accompanies this exemption that many employers and employees fail to take advantage of it. There is a legitimate fear of being in violation of this IRS rule that may cause the taxpayer to run afoul of the government and result in needless penalties.

There is also the problem of what happens if the business owner is late paying the payroll tax. Many small businesses struggle to make payroll and some are late paying employment taxes. The business then becomes liable to pay a penalty and interest on money owed. The employee will receive their federal tax money back (not Social Security Taxes or Medicare Taxes), the government gets to collect penalties and interest, and the employer is the only one who loses. If we remember that the employer is the one who creates jobs then we must eliminate this problem.

The benefits of this proposed IRS change are definitely far reaching. The more pay that lower-end wage earners take home, the better they are able to pay their bills and to be encouraged to save. This helps our economy and our employees. This also helps simplify the employer's payroll and filing, perhaps even reducing the amount they pay to outsource payroll tax processing. It could also mean a reduction in work-load at the government level used to process the tax filings and annual taxpayer refunds.

UNEMPLOYMENT INSURANCE

Unemployment benefits are a necessary ingredient for an economy to avoid wide swings during times of contraction in the economy. With payments from unemployment insurance, displaced employees should be able to continue to make their credit payments and avoid the foreclosure of their homes, repossession of vehicles, and skirt filing bankruptcy. This allows large businesses that must lay off a large population of employees due to market conditions to keep from devastating the communities these employees reside in.

Unfortunately, the way the system is now operating, the employee can get unemployment money even if they were fired. This may be for failing to show up for work or because the job they did was inferior to what was required by the employer. They may have even caused a major accident in which the employer was held financially responsible.

The current rules governing unemployment insurance require that the employer pay for this benefit for the employee. When unemployment insurance is used by the employee, the employer is subject to higher future premiums and the former employee gets paid for a time without having to work. In this scenario, the employee is actually rewarded for his under-performance.

It is not uncommon for individuals to be fired from a job and collect unemployment benefits for a much longer period than is really necessary. They view this as a way of "getting back" at their former employer. After all, they do not pay the premiums for this insurance coverage and therefore, have no stake in hurrying out to find another job.

They are being paid to not work. It is like a well-deserved vacation for having to deal with their previous employer for such a long time, even if it was just a few months. As we have seen with the most recent recession, many of these workers fail to even try to find another job until the time their unemployment runs out.

During this unemployed period they fill out a couple of papers once a week, or even file them online, to keep benefits flowing. Some do try to find other employment or even start their own business, but many more do not. They are not interested in obtaining a job at all. They really just want to take some time off. Why not? During this time they are their own boss. They can sleep late, do what they want when they want, and still collect a check.

We need to change the perception that you can get paid and yet not really try to gain meaningful employ-ment. Until that happens we will continue to see less productivity from unemployment eligible workers.

The immediate need is to evaluate who should receive unemployment benefits. We should consider the incomes of the employees themselves prior to becoming unemployed.

In our society we can generally classify employees into two groups, unskilled and skilled laborers. This distinction is necessary primarily because of the difference in income levels.

Unskilled laborer positions are typically lower paying but also more readily available. In the realm of this job classification I would include convenience store clerks, fast food employees, and some warehouse workers. Since these jobs are more readily available and require no advanced training, I do not feel that it is necessary for unemployment benefits to apply. There are some of these jobs that do pay very well and those workers would be eligible. The defining point would be the annual income level.

The next set of workers make up our skilled workforce. These jobs will usually require a degree, license, or other professional credentialing in order to be employed in that field. Having those requirements usually means that the income level will be higher than that of the unskilled laborers. When a person loses these kinds of jobs it may be more difficult to quickly obtain another job making a similar income. These jobs are ones that should be eligible for unemployment insurance.

We should establish a level of income at which, below that level, the employer would not be required to pay for unemployment insurance and the employee would not be eligible to receive benefits. The rationale for this is that below a certain income level the employee will be able to readily find another job. The new job will typically be around the same income level. Therefore, there would be no need to pay for benefits. I perceive this level to be in the $12,000 to $15,000 annual salary range.

The next thing we must consider is that of not giving unemployment benefits to people who will not work. Since unemployment money is a replacement income for work performed then displaced employees will need to work to collect this money. There are many jobs that our state and federal governments could use these workers for. I offer that if they are not working then they have time to accomplish many tasks that are needing done at the local level.

Each person will be given a schedule, list of duties, and a place of work that they will report to each week. At the end of each week they will receive their unemployment check as compensation for their "job" they have been assigned. They will not be considered employees of the government but will need to work in order to collect a tax-funded check. If they do not show up or are dismissed for failure to perform, then their unemployment checks will cease. It is my belief that if a person will not work or work effectively, then they will not be paid.

Over the long term I believe some big changes will need to occur. If the current system is kept then the above paragraph should be implemented. However, I would like to see us start a shift away from the federal government when it comes to unemployment insurance. It is not the government's responsibility to administer something like this when private companies could do the job more effectively and efficiently. Privatizing unemployment will generate more private sector jobs, produce less government waste, require fewer government employees, and involve much less bureaucracy. For our legislators to begin addressing this issue, they should establish laws that begin to shift responsibility for this type of insurance away from the employer and onto the employee.

In my opinion, excluding contracted positions, it is not the responsibility of any employer to guarantee a job. Neither is it reasonable to expect a business to insure that jobs will remain or that pay will not be affected in the months or years to come. It is the employee's responsibility to protect his or her income so as not to suffer loss during unexpected changes in employment circumstances. We do this with automotive insurance, homeowners insurance, and even renters insurance. If you have a job that pays a decent wage, and you want to insure against a job loss, then you should be able to purchase insurance for that purpose.

In the process of doing this, we would create another product for private insurers which also creates additional jobs in the private sector. In addition, this will provide an incentive for workers to maintain employment even when fired or if they experience a layoff. Workers who have many claims or extended periods of unemployment would be a higher risk client and may not even be insurable. The risk of higher premiums will deter many workers from taking a long hiatus between jobs. This is one proposed policy that will help us get away from the entitlement philosophy that many of our workers have today.

THE NEW ROLE OF EMPLOYEE UNIONS

When I was a Paramedic working for a certain EMS entity, there was a vote to determine whether to allow a union to come in to our facility or not. During this time there was much debate and over-and-over I was told of things that had happened to previous employees. It was because of those stories that I voted to allow the union. This action succeeded and I believe it was a good thing for all employees involved.

So why do I think there should be a new role for unions? It was not necessarily pay that was being challenged at this job, although that was part of it. My pay was actually frozen because my starting salary was higher than what many other employees were making – even some who had been with the company for 7 to 9 years. They were in the same category I was with much more experience making significantly less than me. This was not right and although it affected me negatively to vote for the union, I felt it was the right thing to do.

This was not the only problem. Many employees were reprimanded or fired and had no significant voice when they felt they were being targeted. The union was able to give that voice to the employees and allowed for a more formal process of discipline. The rules were spelled out for both management and workers and representation was equal to both sides.

This is the role I believe unions need to take. The era of dictating higher pay and benefits is long gone. This is because we no longer compete in an American economy - we compete in a world economy. Our workers compete with workers from China, India, Japan, and other developed and developing nations.

To be competitive, the pay and benefits provided by employers must be able to flex depending on what is happening with its competitors worldwide. The days of expecting excellent pay and benefits for work that can be done in another country for several times less cannot continue to exist.

Employers must be able to remain dynamic, responsive to economic trends, and profitable. If our unions hamper the ability of the company to respond to these worldwide pressures, the businesses will most assuredly move their operations to other countries in order to survive.

We see this trend by noting that there are fewer union workers in the private sector today. This is due to having many unionized industries closing or moving their operations. Companies had finally decided they could no longer offer the benefits and wages being insisted on by the unions. They chose instead to relocate to other countries. We must reverse this trend.

The unions I envision are there to protect workers from unfair labor practices. They have no say in the pay and benefits offered to employees as long as those things are fairly administered to all employees. For instance, management would be prohibited from offering certain benefits to some employees and withholding those same benefits from other employees who are doing the same job. Pay based on merit would be allowed but arbitrary pay raises or cuts would not be allowed.

The days of the union demanding increased pay and benefits based on the success of the business is long gone. Look around and see how many unionized jobs still exist. How many of those companies have relocated leaving behind bone yards of the glory days? How many people in those areas have had to settle for jobs paying much less just to get by? They remember the times when the company was running strong, employing hundreds, and now they are wishing that the employer was still around.

Would it not be better to have that company local, hiring your friends and family, anchoring communities together, and improving the infrastructure of our towns? Let's start by revamping our idea of what the role of unions should be.

LIMITS ON INTEREST RATES

Over the last several decades the credit card issuers have succeeded in becoming a mainstay in the economy. The lender's extension of credit to individuals has increased the consumer's purchasing power. This credit increase allows consumers to have buying power that is several times over what they would be able to afford by paying cash. Payday cash advances and used car resellers have taken to using some of the same tactics in order to sell their services or products to make a profit.

This all works because of the desire of so many Americans to own what they cannot afford. In order to extend this credit and be able to weather the losses that are sure to come, the credit issuers charge exorbitantly high interest rates. It is no longer uncommon to see credit card interest rates at 20% and even 30% on new purchases.

When we look at this extension of credit we must not forget that it skews the supply-demand cycle. It artificially creates an increased demand coupled with an influx of money that results in escalating prices. That demand will slow when credit limits are reached, money stops flowing from the creditors into the economy, and defaults begin to rise. Unfortunately, since the rise in demand was built on this "borrowed" money it takes a long time for the repossession, rebuilding, and spending phase to cycle through.

Excessive interest payments are major factors that limit the amount of discretionary income a person has to spend. Paychecks are consumed paying interest on previous purchases and therefore cannot be used to buy other items.

High interest rates are argued for by credit issuers in order to absorb the defaults that occur in the industry. Without those higher rates the credit issuers may need to refuse credit to those who are higher credit risks. I would argue that this is not a bad idea. When you have credit issuers who target low-income individuals or people with bad credit, are they not taking advantage of those people and their situation? This becomes an ethical question and one that can be argued. However, I believe that we should not subject people of limited means or those who have proven an inability to manage their credit well to the trap of high interest rate loans.

How we control these interest rates is not very difficult. Credit interest rates should be tied to a certain financial benchmark much like an adjustable rate mortgage. The maximum rate can then be determined based on the rate of that financial instrument. In today's economic climate, I see the maximum interest rate around 15% for unsecured credit and somewhere around 10% for secured credit. Credit issuers can compete below the maximum rate but not above it. If this rate prevents a credit issuer from extending credit to certain individuals because the risk of default is higher than the profit expected, then that individual probably does not need the credit anyway.

If this policy is implemented, I can see a significant and rapid improvement in discretionary income for individuals around the country. This will translate into more purchasing power immediately for consumers and a dramatic infusion of money back into our economy. This will be real money that has been earned, not borrowed money.

I also see fewer bankruptcies and less defaults as less credit is extended. People will actually own what they possess instead of just "borrowing" it from the bank, finance company, or other credit issuer. My desire is that we will see Americans saving more and being better stewards of the money they make.

HOME MORTGAGES

Home ownership is one of the great things we have in America. With the downturn in the economy and many foreclosures we have the opportunity to see where we went wrong and try to make corrections. We do not want to have to again experience the kind of real estate recession we are experiencing today.

One of the most egregious areas of mortgages I have seen is in the "Introductory Rates" that permeated the market before the collapse. The mortgage amount and payments were figured using a below market introductory rate that would expire at some point in the future. This enabled sellers to price and sell their houses higher as more people qualified for higher mortgages using this scheme.

For instance, the borrowers may not have been able to afford the payment on a $200,000 home at a normal interest rate yet, with an incredibly low rate they would. This allowed borrowers to spend more for a house because their payments would be less. However, when the mortgage rate adjusted many homeowners found out they could not afford the new payment.

Our government needs to prohibit "Introductory Rates" on mortgages. This should not be allowed on any home mortgage, whether a first home or a second home. Not only does it affect the payment but it also affects the home values for other buyers.

The next thing I would like to see with primary home mortgages is an overall reduction in the length of mortgages from 30-year amortizations to 20-year amortizations for primary residences. There are two reasons I would like to bring this to the table for consideration.

The mortgage payments are of negligible differences between a 20-year and a 30-year note but the interest savings are tremendous. On a home mortgaged for $50,000, the principle and interest payment on a 30-year loan at 6% would be $299.78. The same loan amount and interest for a 20-year loan would be $358.22. On a $125,000 loan, a 30-year amortized mortgage would equate to $749.44 per month and on a 20-year amortization, $895.54 per month..

If we do this, we cannot discount the effect of the more rapid increase in home equity for the homeowners. The peak earning years are around 40-50 years old for most Americans. Imagine that you purchase a home at 50 years old and you will be paying on it until your 80 years old. I submit that you do not know what your health will be like at that time or whether you will even be able to live in the home until that age. There is a good chance, based on current demographics, that you may need extensive medical care or even be moved to a nursing home or assisted-living center. If you are 70 years old, retired, and still have ten years left to pay on your mortgage, how will you continue to pay it and your other medical and living expenses? Yet, if you paid the home off in 20 years you would have it free-and-clear. This situation will allow you to draw more money from the equity through a reverse mortgage, a sale of the home, or you may even allow yourself the option to keep the home and pass it on to your heirs.

To bring home loans down to 20 years we must be careful not to adversely affect current home values. This must be done in a slow and orderly fashion. This 20-year amortization law will not affect second homes, only primary residences.

My recommendation is to decrease the maximum home mortgage length by two years every three years. The first adjustment would result in a maximum 28-year loan for the first year. Three years later the maximum loan will be for 26 years. Three years later it would be for 24 years and so on. This would take a long time but could be accelerated to an every-two-year adjustment period if it is felt by economists that home values will not decrease significantly. One thing we must do is preserve the value current homeowners have in their property. Too rapid of a decrease may negatively affect them and lead to a prolongation of the real estate recession. However, it could be argued that a rapid decrease, especially in our current economic climate, would be best since home values are already down and may not decrease much more.

An extra benefit to homeowners is they will build equity more quickly in a home by paying much less interest over the length of the loan. This should help consumers have more buying power over the course of their lives. When we consider that homeowners will pay more than $100,000 in mortgage interest, in many cases significantly more, I have to believe that money would be better spent in the local economy.

With this extra stability among our American citizens I believe we can expect more stability in our economy. This should also translate into a more resilient American dollar and a more fiscally sound government.

CREDIT PROTECTION

Credit profiling has been used to such a great extent that incorrect data can affect the creditworthiness of individuals who would otherwise be considered acceptable credit risks. Some of these include cases where identity theft has caused delinquencies, late pays, etc. to affect the credit report of the victim. The onus is put on the victim to resolve the issue.

Credit reporting agencies are paid for this information. Businesses then use this information to determine the creditworthiness of their customers. This exchange of information is valuable. Unfortunately, the reporting that is made, if erroneous, leads to complications for an individual in a way that does not affect either the businesses or the credit reporting agencies. To be fair to consumers, the information needs to be correct.

The businesses and the credit reporting agencies must provide accurate information concerning every person. The Federal Trade Commission should provide consumer advocacy in matters where inaccurate information is displayed as part of their credit file.

Before submitting information to a credit reporting agency, the businesses must take reasonable action to insure that the person they are reporting on is the person who created the debt. Businesses providing inaccurate information to a credit reporting agency will be subject to a fine.

Credit reporting agencies may use information based on the report submitted by a business. If the credit reporting agency discovers that the debt has not been reported correctly, or has been challenged by the consumer, then they must remove the item in question from the report immediately. They must notify the business reporting the item and notify the FTC of the discrepancy. Failure of the credit reporting agency to remove the item in dispute will subject the agency to a daily fine until the information is removed.

If the item is removed from the credit reporting profile and the business has been notified, then the business should then try to ascertain the correct information. If the business cannot verify that the debt was created by the person contesting the information then they must refrain from submitting it to the credit reporting agency in the future. If the business verifies that the correct information has been submitted, then the credit reporting agency may re-list it on their reports. More particulars can be discussed in the state legislatures concerning the rights of the consumer and when a re-listing may occur.

The goal is to prevent identity theft from adversely affecting the consumer in a more effective way than we have established here-to-date. The burden will shift to the businesses reporting and to the credit reporting agencies listing the information. It will move away from the consumers having to spend a great deal of time and money to prove that a debt does not belong to them. The businesses that benefit from such reports will need to make sure the information contained in such a report is accurate. A financial consequence will help persuade companies to make their reports accurate.

SPOUSAL FINANCIAL OBLIGATIONS

In many states only one spouse is needed to obligate both parties to a debt. This may be done completely without the consent of the other spouse yet both are on the hook to repay the debt. In the distant past, debt was created sparingly, only one spouse worked outside of the home, and credit extended to consumers was much more limited. Today, both spouses work, credit is readily available, and many times one spouse will obligate the family to massive debt without the consent of the other party.

With divorce rates in the U.S. at such a high level and no sign that it will get better, we must reconsider how we take care of this issue. Taking some minor precautions will keep the actions of one spouse from affecting the credit worthiness of the other spouse. It will also prevent the income from a non-consenting spouse to be used to secure credit for the other spouse.

The law should be changed to reflect that any financial obligation that is created is the sole responsibility of the signing party. The credit issuer or financial institution will need to verify that the signatures of the applicants are authentic and not forgeries. This could be as simple as requiring a Notary verification or other means of establishing an identity. Without this verification the credit issuer will have no legal basis for trying to secure payment from the non-signer.

A little more complex issue is that of a married couple who is saving funds for the future. Many times marriage is composed of a spender and a saver. When divorce happens the money that is saved is then split between the parties involved. However, we must consider that in today's world, there are usually two working adults and both are bringing incomes into the marriage. If the saver has managed their funds well and the spender has not, then there should not be an automatic obligation for those funds to be split. The court should be given the discretion to distribute those funds in a way that more fairly represents the saving habits of the one spouse. This is where the court needs to be given a little more latitude in those states where marital property is just split equally.

INCREASING THE SAVINGS RATE OF AMERICANS

It is well documented that Americans are not saving very much of their income and actually have very little, if any, emergency cash available for unexpected expenses. This has caused more consumers to rely on credit to meet routine expenses and has weakened their ability to respond to a crisis.

On a global scale, this has weakened the strength of the American dollar. The value of the American dollar to investors is based on the ability of our country to repay the loans we have created. These are debts that we have generally created by issuing bonds. If the perceived ability to repay a bond becomes questionable, then interest rates for bonds increase. This means that future borrowing will result in more of the repayment going to pay interest instead of principle and thus, require more tax money.

Part of the solution to this problem is to convince consumers to put more money into savings and to rely less on loans, especially credit card loans. It is my opinion that as the common man manages his finances well, the more he will expect our elected officials to do the same with his tax dollars.

The American consumer will be an integral part of increasing the value of the dollar. The amount of savings the average person has is vital to this cause. I am convinced there are many people who will do this if they know what to do. The focus will need to be on education that gives them specific goals to attain.

Public Service Announcements should tout the benefits of having an emergency savings account of at least $1,000. Banks should encourage savings through the development of new cash reserve instruments. Financial education should be taught at both the high school and college levels stressing the importance of long term savings.

Along with this, there will be the need to reduce credit card interest rates and shorten loan periods so that borrowed money is repaid quicker. This will result in the ability of the consumer to resume a savings strategy. The Federal Government also needs to balance the budget and to repay loans so that we are not indebted to other nations. The borrower is servant to the lender and America needs to be a lender and a leader, not a servant.

I am thoroughly convinced that if our dollar is not strengthened, and our state and federal governments continue to encourage deficit spending, we will cease to be a powerful player in the world. Our state and federal governments should be virtually debt-free. The U.S. needs to be a fiscally strong nation and not a weak, indebted people.

.

I believe that when American citizens start to save instead of spend on credit, we will see more account-ability in our government. This will have the effect of greatly increasing the status of America around the world as the strength of our dollar increases and our debt is paid off. Bonds we issue will be at reduced interest rates and we will be less subject to global instabilities. As a bonus, stock in American companies will increase in value and be less volatile to global economic changes.

ENTITLEMENT PROGRAMS IN GENERAL

Entitlement programs at their core are designed to help those who cannot help themselves. It is no secret that there are many individuals who are unable to take care of themselves because of various diseases or handicaps. I believe that most of these people should be helped at the local level by caring people who understand their particular situation and can address specific issues as they arise. There are many nonprofit entities, churches, and help organizations that have been created for just such purposes.

Should people who are unable to provide for themselves be solely reliant on those organizations for help? Many advocate that, but I worry about scenarios where those in need of help are taken advantage of because of their reliance on a particular local organization. Most of these help organizations are very good but it only takes one bad apple to sour all the good.

In order to alleviate some of this concern for abuse, I support the continuation of federal and state money to be used with various government programs. This will allow the beneficiary to have some money in their pockets so they are not totally reliant on a local organization.

Here is where we run into problems with the government help programs. There are too many people who are capable of working and providing for themselves, and their families, but they choose not to do so. With so

45

many give-away programs and such lenient criteria for qualifying, we are seeing many of these good programs abused. We have generations who look for these entitlement programs for themselves, their parents, and now their children. Just like "welfare" from times past, people search for ways to get paid without having to work for it. The working people of this nation are subject to seeing their tax dollars wasted on people who are too lazy to work. The reasoning becomes, "Why do I have to work when I will lose this money I am already receiving?". This system, as it is currently designed, entraps many people into a lifestyle of being provided for without working for it.

So many people are on government benefits and almost daily we see those who are abusing the system. I feel that such a large amount of the money committed to government help programs is wasted on fraud. Eliminating that misuse of funds will result in a tremendous amount of available monies that could be used more appropriately.

The most important thing we can do, and by far the easiest thing to do, is weed out the fraud that is occur-ring in these government programs. I suggest the hiring of investigators at the state level to find the fraud and help eliminate it. In my state, Arkansas, I would like to see a department with four investigators, a secretary, Director, and a Judge assigned to the department.

The investigators will go out and in essence, catch those who are doing the things they should not be able to do while receiving benefits. Many of these people I am talking about are on SSI Disability. If they are on disability for back problems then they should not be able to carry firewood or lift a beer cooler into a boat.

A video would be shot of them doing these things and then sent to the secretary who prepares a "Discontinuation of State Benefits" package for the Director. The Director will then issue a letter to the person committing the alleged fraud notifying them of the immediate discontinuation of all state benefits. The Director would then schedule a hearing for the following week with the assigned Judge. The person will be given the opportunity to defend their actions. If they lose their case or fail to show for the hearing, the state will withhold all future benefits for a period of not less than thirty years, or age seventy, whichever is later. The reasoning is this, in lieu of prosecution and jail time, which will cost the taxpayers more, suspending future benefits will save the taxpayers money. Even if at some point in the future, if the accused qualifies before that time has expired, there will be nothing the government will do. This person will be on their own as punishment for scamming the system in the first place.

The results of the state process will then be forwarded to federal authorities who would take the same approach to cease benefits in the same manner. The state and federal governments should be very vigilant to protect taxpayer dollars. Anyone on government assistance is subject to increased scrutiny in order to limit fraud.

Along with eliminating fraud we must also redesign our current system that entraps people into entitlement mentalities. When I was around 17 years of age I had a plan that I advocated then and now still consider it to be viable – with maybe a few tweaks.

A person who needs extensive help would be placed on a maximum five-year plan. During this time they would be eligible for living money, childcare, food allowances, and other services. They would also be eligible for tuition money and be required to gain a degree or learn a trade. Depending on the circumstances, the amount of assistance will be adjusted but should require, in most cases, that the beneficiary be employed in addition to going to school. Once finished with their degree or have learned their trade, they will be given one year, as long as it is within the five-year period, in order to be weaned from government assistance. Letters would be sent out at one-year, six-month, three-month, and one-month periods notifying the recipient of termination of the program. This will allow them more than enough time to adjust to their current income level. After that point, the person should be able to support them-selves without government assistance and would be prohibited from collecting further benefits for a significant amount of time, perhaps twenty years or so.

There are many plans, and many good plans, that can be designed to help with this gigantic problem. In the end, it must be understood that we, American taxpayers, cannot continue to pay people not to work.

We must also realize that this extra government money actually skews the supply-demand paradigm by creating increased demand and thus increasing prices. These increased prices often lead to higher government funding of entitlement programs because of the increased costs. This begins spiraling prices higher and higher.

Undoing this cycle that has been created over several decades will require a steady but planned response. The goal is to eliminate government funding without taking so much out of the economy too rapidly that we cause another recession-like atmosphere. However, to not do this will only weaken the future prosperity of our country.

AMENDING LEGAL LIABILITY LAWS IN HEALTH CARE

It has been apparent for many years that there needs to be a limit to legal liability for those involved in providing health care to Americans. Because of the limitless liability amounts that can be imposed, health care premiums for insurance coverage have gone up tremendously. This often puts coverage out of reach for many consumers. In addition, costs for hospitalizations and evaluations have significantly increased since physicians must practice lawsuit-preventive medicine. This type of guarded practice causes physicians to order extra treatments and tests that they may know, or generally presume, will not benefit the patient. However, they feel that they must do them just to cover all bases to prevent a lawsuit. These costs are passed on to the consumer as higher treatment costs and higher insurance premiums.

State legislatures need to establish liability amounts based on the severity of the injury. The amounts of compensation may be negotiated in the legislatures but there should be a maximum liability per person. All amounts that may be listed do not include the cost of reasonable legal fees and the original billed amount of services rendered. I envision something to the effect of $500,000 as the maximum amount of liability that could be awarded to a plaintiff. This type of compensation would be awarded in cases resulting in the death or permanent disability of the patient.

Maximum limits for other situations would be less than that amount and apply to cases such as improper surgical procedures, infections due to poor sterilization techniques, or other faulted causes. Those amounts would need to be decided at the state level. Certain types of cases can be grouped together and will have set maximum amounts assigned to them. Juries will be able to decide to award claims at or below those maximum amounts.

To help prevent shotgun approaches to filing these lawsuits we must require that the liable party be identified. If a surgeon makes a mistake during surgery then the physician is to be held liable. The hospital and staff will be free from having to defend their actions and may not be sued. If the patient develops an infection from something in the hospital and not from the physician, then the hospital may be sued and not the physician. If a nurse causes harm then the nurse may be sued and not the hospital or physician. It seems that so many cases try to make a defendant out of everyone who had anything at all to do with the patient. This only results in the loss of productivity for the wrongfully accused. Therefore, it should be required that only the party who may be reasonably identified as most likely liable may be able to be sued.

Implementing both of these measures should produce an almost immediate savings to the hospitals and other facilities providing health care to consumers. Resources will be able to be utilized based on need instead of used to prevent a lawsuit. This should also lead to lower premiums for hospital liability insurance, physician liability insurance, and lower premiums for consumer health care insurance. With unnecessary procedures and tests eliminated, the consumer should see a reduction in health care expenses. They will not be paying for things that increase the bill without having much of a diagnostic benefit. Even though there are catastrophic things that do occur and $500,000 does not even come close to compensation, we must consider the entire health care system and not the few people that may be negatively affected by this.

INABILITY TO PAY MEDICAL BILLS

Due to the high cost of health care, many consumers who seek medical attention find that the bills that
follow are often much more than they can afford. It is not
typically an unwillingness to pay but an inability to pay.
These consumers receive bills from many providers such
as the hospital, radiologists, and anesthesiologists, but
often do not have the means to pay them. If those bills
are reported to a credit reporting agency, the effects can
be devastating to otherwise financially responsible
people. This will affect their ability to purchase a home,
car, and can prevent them from obtaining a job. In my
experience, this is not a sign of the persons irre-
sponsibility to manage financial purchases, but a case of
uncontrollable circumstances that can plague them for
years to come.

A consumers may be very good, financially
speaking, but may suddenly become ill. They may seek
medical attention, recover, and yet have a very large bill.
They may not have the means to repay this new debt and
continue paying the other bills that were already part of
their budget. This may result in slow payments or even a
default of the amount owed.

A law that prevents health care providers,
including hospitals, doctors, nursing homes, etc., from
reporting to a credit reporting agency would be the most
effective way to prevent this from happening. Providers
may still attempt to collect the debt and work with the
consumer on a payment plan. This will not affect the

rights of the businesses from taking legal action against the consumer in order to rectify the debt.

We must consider that the consumer did not go out and intentionally become ill or injured. It is not like going to buy a boat, car, or other planned expense. We must not allow this experience to affect their financial picture for a great number of years. This simple law can keep a previously good credit risk from becoming a bad credit risk for something he or she may not have had control over.

ATTORNEY CONTINGENCY AGREEMENTS

It is a common practice for attorneys to accept cases on contingency of payment based on winning the case. It may be that if the case is won, the attorney will collect all expenses associated plus one-third of the remaining settlement. If the arrangement is similar to this, many consumers will see little if any of the settlement because of the way this is structured.

An attorney is a professional and charges fees for their service. Physicians also charge for their services and are generally held to usual and customary charges by insurance companies. I believe there should be a guide for attorneys as well. A department within the State Attorney General's office should develop a "usual and customary" charge guide for use in the state.

When an attorney chooses to take on a case with a contingency, he or she will only be able to bill for services at the rate assigned by the Attorney General. If the case is won, those charges will be subtracted from the settlement amount along with a detailed list of expenses incurred, a copy of those charges submitted to the plaintiff (or defendant in cases of a counter-suit) and a copy submitted to the Attorney General's office along with other pertinent required documents.

I also believe that a maximum percentage limit should be imposed on contingency cases. To receive one-third of the settlement after charges are subtracted seems predatory to me. A maximum of a 10% contingency fee

57

seems much more reasonable. The compensation routine would go something like this: upon winning the case, the attorney will collect his expenses and customary fee and may obtain a maximum of 10% of the remaining settlement. For example, a plaintiff sues and wins $10,000 in the settlement. The attorney documents usual and customary expenses in the amount of $2,500. His fee allowed per the Attorney General's office is $2,500. The amount of settlement remaining is $5,000. The attorney is allowed to charge 10%, or $500, for his contingency fee. $4,500 is remaining for the plaintiff.

Implementing this policy should reduce the vulture-like atmosphere surrounding contingency lawsuits where only the attorney benefits. It also empowers the plaintiff to know that the fees charged by the attorney are not excessive. Non-contingent lawsuits would not be affected and may still be charged at the client-attorney agreed upon rates.

CAPITAL PUNISHMENT

When we are looking for ways to improve how our taxpayer dollars are spent we must consider the amount we spend to keep criminals locked up in taxpayer funded institutions. It is often argued that capital punishment cases costs the taxpayers so much that we should do away with the practice and look more to "life in prison without the possibility of parole". I do not agree with this at all. The taxpayers continue to be footing the bill for the continued and increasing costs of incarcerations which only rise throughout the lifetime of the prisoner.

I do believe in our American system of justice and the basis that a person is innocent until proven guilty. That is a bedrock of law we must strive to keep in place. However, there are many cases in which the defendant is guilty and there is no question of his or her guilt. This may be a crime in which there were witnesses, video footage, or other means of identification that links the defendant as the perpetrator. We all know and can quickly point to cases where this is applicable. When these cases go to trial, and capital punishment is what is called for, then there should be no need to prolong the process. There should be a designation by prosecutors that this case will be "fast-tracked" for enforcing the punishment. At this point the execution date will be set for no later than 90 days after conviction unless delayed by the courts for unusual circumstances. The appeals process will be required to be completed within this 90 day period and preparations made to carry out the execution at the end of that period. To reiterate, these are cases which require no piecing together of the evidence to point to the defendant – cases in which the defendant is the known perpetrator.

The other capital cases will proceed as normal through the court system with some changes. The legislature should aim for capital punishment cases to be carried out within 360 days of conviction. This usually allows ample time to appeal the decision and have any convictions overturned or obtain a pardon from the Governor. I do favor that the utmost care be done to prevent the execution of an innocent individual. However, I do not feel that prolonging death sentences for decades, in most cases, accomplishes this. Changing these rules will be more of a deterrent to crime and will reduce the amount taxpayers pay to incarcerate these individuals who commit the most heinous crimes.

Many of these ideas are different from what we as an American society are used to. We have demonized businesses for so many decades and have put so many regulations in place that we actually have come to think that many of these policies are normal. The innovations of our early history helps us to understand that we have to let businesses succeed. It is what the "American Dream" was all about.

I have often compared our economy to driving a car. Innovation is the accelerator and regulation is the braking system. For our economy to go forward we must step on the accelerator. More innovation pushes us faster and our economy surges ahead. But, every vehicle must also have a way to slow down. There are curves, bumps, and caution areas that require us to put on the brakes. A runaway car can cause a lot of damage and an economy that does not make adjustments for various situations will face dire consequences. However, more-and-more regulations keep braking the economy to a point where it can come to a complete stop. When this happens we have to spend more time, energy, and resources to get started again. Our fuel mileage is hindered and it takes longer to get back up to speed.

We must stop pushing on the brakes of our economy. We must reduce regulations on businesses. We have come to a stop and it will take time and energy to correct this situation and get rolling again.

We must push for innovation among our citizens and encourage our people to succeed. We must get back to a good work ethic. This is a simple principle that says if you work hard, you will meet the needs of your family and be able to get ahead. We must make it possible for our people to pursue their dreams of success.

Finally, we must stop paying people not to work. Unlike what we have been teaching in our schools for many years, not everyone who shows up to the game wins. Living in the U.S. is not an acceptable criteria for receiving handouts at the expense of the taxpayers. The ones who apply themselves will benefit and those who don't will fall behind.

There are other valuable things we can do in addition to these mentioned. There are great ideas out there that others have thought of and several I have not presented. The goal of this book is to get people thinking outside of the box, generate truly unique ideas, set some goals, and start restoring America to its former glory. May God bless the U.S.A.

ABOUT THE AUTHOR

As a citizen of the United States, I am concerned with the direction our country has taken. I see the great challenges that we must contend with in order to maintain our supremacy in the world. I know we can measure up to the calling to restore our place as a true leader of freedom and ingenuity.

I am a small business owner who faces the challenges associated with hiring employees and meeting federal and state requirements. I am an employee who sees his tax dollars going to support many people who refuse to go to work because our government, using our tax dollars, gives them our money in order to feed and take care of their family. I am an investor who is concerned about the devaluation of our American dollar as the standard for world monetary policy. I am a real estate investor who is still struggling in this lackluster real estate market. I am a Christian who loves the Lord Jesus Christ. I am a father, a brother, and a son.

You see, I am like many of you. We want to be able to succeed here in America but the problem is that there are so many things in place today that hinder our ability to succeed. We see that those who work hard don't get any farther ahead than those who refuse to work. We ask ourselves "why" and the answer is, our government allows them to sit on the couch all day and our tax dollars pay them to do so. It is not fair to those of us who are willing to go out everyday and earn a living only to find that we could have stayed at home and been just as well off. We must go back and find where we went down the wrong path in this country and change it.

I am also a believer that we, as Americans, can accomplish anything if we work together to solve our problems. Many of these issues are not Republican or Democrat issues. Yes, some are conservative issues but they are also economically sound issues. My hope is that you will read this book, make notes, and then get involved helping to change our country for the better. May God richly bless you.

Damon D. Wallace

Contact:
Damon D. Wallace
P.O. Box 137
Bentonville, AR 72712
or
LinkedIn & Facebook